Black L♥ve

D1521596

Black L♥ve

A Book of Poetry & Love

Alice V. Benton

iUniverse, Inc.
New York Lincoln Shanghai

Black Love
A Book of Poetry & Love

iUniverse books may be ordered through booksellers or by contacting:

iUniverse
2021 Pine Lake Road, Suite 100
Lincoln, NE 68512
www.iuniverse.com
1-800-Authors (1-800-288-4677)

Because of the dynamic nature of the Internet, any Web addresses or links contained in this book may have changed since publication and may no longer be valid.

The views expressed in this work are solely those of the author and do not necessarily reflect the views of the publisher, and the publisher hereby disclaims any responsibility for them.

ISBN: 978-0-595-44750-3 (pbk)
ISBN: 978-0-595-89071-2 (ebk)

Printed in the United States of America

To God be the Glory!

I dedicate this love story represented through poetry to all my loved ones, especially my parents, siblings and their children, particularly my sister Jennifer (may she rest in peace) and the incident that eventually inspired me to truly live.

Jennifer

Everyday I am missing you
Your presence
A blessing
Your absence
An ever-changing void

Special thanks to Doc Hollywood for serving as a catalyst of Black Love

Extra Special thanks to Angelika for telling me to stay true to the books original form & Arabia for naming a few of the poems—Girls thank you for allowing me to love more than I ever knew I could. You are two great sources of inspiration in my everyday life and are always supportive of me. You mean the world to me.

My Girls

You are wonderfully separate
Although an important part of me
Daily you impress me
Being wildly independent
And wise beyond your years
I have learned much
Through your love
I have nurtured you
And yet we have raised each other
I see
Intelligence, beauty & Great Spirit
You humble me
Thank you
For a priceless legacy
God has shown favor on me
Through you—my girls

Contents

Introduction . . . . *xi*

Why . . . . *xiii*

<u>Guy 1</u>—*The Beginning*

Waking Up 3

Making Love 4

The Man I Love 5

Seeing You 6

<u>Guy 2</u>—*Distant Lover*

Still 9

Touch Me 10

Touching You 11

How 12

Tomorrow 13

<u>Guy 3</u>—*Distractions*

Untitled I 17

Untitled II 18

True Blessings 19

Bleeding Heart *20*

It Was Never Love *21*

Guy 4—Revelations

More of the Same *25*

Why You're So Important. *26*

Last Night. *27*

Aching Soul. *28*

The Dance *30*

Pain *32*

Change. *34*

Guy 5—Awakening

It *37*

Love *38*

Best Friend. *39*

Good Love. *40*

God's Gift. *41*

Inspiration *42*

Heaven. *43*

Your Love *44*

Conclusion *46*

Appreciation *47*

Poem Index. *49*

Picture Index *51*

Introduction

Black Love—A Book of Poetry & Love is about my personal experiences with love. I do not love freely, but when I do I love completely, so welcome to my soul. I have encountered a great deal in my life, from one extreme to another. The following poems are an intense description of how I have felt along the way. If you are anything like me, this book will give you access to poetry that you can truly feel, while relating to and sharing with another.

It has taken me a while, but I finally know that a relationship should be a positive and nurturing experience that does your soul good while contributing to its growth. True love does not and cannot go away. It is an ever-constant source of energy that always provides support and reassurance. If you are living in a relationship where negativity resides and need to reconnect, find a way to remember that real love begins inside ones self. It is important to never forget just how important you are, as I have at times. The following poem, *Why*, is my daily reminder:

Introduction Picture by Marie Ostensson

Why

Because I breathe
I am important
Because my Lord allowed me to wake
I am great
As I continue to wake
I shall continue to be great
And each moment I live I am blessed
As I get older
I will get better
Because my God has faith in me
Faith to cherish the life He has given

Guy One

The Beginning

The Beginning

Waking Up

When I wake up
It's different
And when I say different
I mean
I feel that no one else has ever experienced what I do
They wake up to the world
I wake up to you
You are my world
In your eyes I see love
In your voice I hear passion
You are like the moon
Always there but transparent at times
And the stars that brighten up the darkest nights
You are as important to me as the sun is to the universe
You are my life

Making Love

It begins with a touch
Powerful yet gentle
Filled with deep love and undying passion
Yes
Please touch me over and over again
Our eyes meet
Yours filled with complete ecstasy
Mine with satisfaction
Finally
I feel your love
Intimately
And deep within me
Hours later
It shall end with a kiss
Because when he kisses me I am in heaven
And I will remain in heaven
As we sleep

The Man I Love

He is a gift
Or at least he was
He loves me
Yet he hurts me
He hurts me more than he shows his love
He hurts me so much I feel abused
Although he has never hit me
He sounds like he wants to
He looks like he wants to
Existing, wandering, hoping, praying
I am ready to walk away
Then he looks at me
Through me
In me
So sweet, loving, caring
All the things I love

Seeing You

Seeing you is wonderful
I saw you tonight
And you inspired me
You inspired me in a way that sparked intense feelings
And those feelings
Manifest in a dream
Hmmm …
My dream was beautiful
The daily anxieties that plague me
Were kissed away and replaced with multiple satisfactions
Seeing you was wonderful
And I am ready
To see you again

Guy Two

Distant Lover

Distant Love

Still

He is no longer distant
He is close
I see him all the time
And still long for him
I touch him
Repeatedly
And still … I am in love with him
The love continues to grow
His touch
Excitable
My skin yearns for it
The intense undertone of his voice
Hmmm, it commands things of my soul
And yes … he will have what he wants
He is my King
And will be until the end of time
He is everything
And I thank him
Thank you, for showing, no, reminding me that I am a Queen

Touch Me

Touch me lover
Touch me with those lips I love
Those lips that suck me with increasing desire
Introduce your tongue to me ... slowly
That tongue that licks me
Those hands that caress my body
Our body, as soft or hard as it needs
Allow me to feel all your flesh against mine
Stare deep into my eyes as we explode
Your eyes at that moment are filled with intense happiness
Your look stays with me
Thank you for a great morning memory

Touching You

Touching you is heaven
Every time I look at you
I see and feel love
My love embraces you exquisitely
It was made for you
You romance me more than I thought possible
Touching you is ecstasy
You are forever a part of my soul

How

How will I sleep?
Turning to see you
Feel you
Love you
How will I relax?
Knowing my angel
Is away
Knowing my piece of heaven
Is gone
I will wait for you
Even though
I cannot wait
To feel heaven around me once more

Tomorrow

Tomorrow
Can begin today
By making a simple decision
We may choose to love one another
Not because it is a choice
Instead we choose because
Our lives need it
For that reason
Today
I have decided
To love you
In all of my tomorrows
I choose to love you
In every moment
Of every day
In every breath I take

Guy Three

Distractions

Distractions

Untitled 1

Too many men have hurt me
And then there you were
You restored my faith
By the eloquent way you talk
And interact with all
You are truly amazing
I would close my eyes
And listen intensely
For your every breath
Just to feel your essence upon me
Your everything
Does my soul good
I thank you for that
I thank you
For allowing me to feel something
Anything
Other than pain

Untitled 2

A night so perfect
Time flew
Your kiss
Better than imagined
We shared the same passionate dream
I became alive in ways never felt before
Even while you were simply holding me
Just the thought of next time gave me satisfaction

True Blessings

What happened to the bond
I thought we shared
We were there not me
Right?
We were vibin' and chillin'
And doin' our thing
Then suddenly without warning the love was gone
It's all good but I'm confused
Never before was I used & abused
I want the answer you refuse to supply
So instead I had to ask my Lord why
He told me
I had been blessed
A man shook so fast only brings stress
So I thank God for playing this hand
My eyes have been opened
I know where I stand

Bleeding Heart

My heart is bleeding for you
This heart that use to flow to a smooth and beautiful tempo
The pace now ragged
It spills over in pain
Pain that shutters through every inch of my being
You once helped it flow peacefully
You once catered to it
Now
You have pierced my forever bleeding heart

It Was Never Love

He never loved me
I think I knew somehow
I wanted him to love me
Perhaps, I felt I needed him to love me
And still, it was never love
When words are all you have
It is not love
When actions or the lack of actions consume you
It is not love
When you are blamed for all the bad in his life
It is not love
And it was never love
How does a man look at you and say
I love you
I'm in love with you
And not have a need to call
Not need to include you in his life
Not need to see or touch you
Not think to include you for a minute during important events
I'm certain he shares with those he loves
Maybe it was something
But it was never love
I should have protected myself
Guarded my mind, heart & body

I see the truth now
Thank God, but I'm alone again
No, still because it was never love

Guy Four

Revelations

Revelations

More of the Same

I thought I learned something
I felt ... better
I thought ...
If I could <u>act</u> right
I would deserve ...
No, receive some goodness
You made me <u>want</u> to be good
So I was ... yes, was
No wonder people are so bad
It doesn't seem to matter how <u>good</u> you are
Well, there goes that ...
Cheers!
Here's to a new day

Why You're So Important

We talk
We not only listen
We share
We are intimate
Intimate in a way that no one understands
We have told each other things
Without speaking a word
You're important because you've become a part of me
Thank you

Last Night

I spoke to you last night
But I didn't
My unspoken breath told you things
That my lips could not
I know you heard me
But you choose not to question it
Maybe you should have
We lingered
Hoping
Waiting
Wanting
Our friendship is too great
So I let you sleep
I will cherish you always
But last night made me wish we never became friends

Aching Soul

My soul aches without you
It's rustling with my being
Fighting to get out of this physical misery
It's trapped in this pain
How could you have messed with my very existence?
Disturbing me to my core
We are connected
I feel you at a glance
Every time I blink I feel you
You're in my mind
You have taken over my heart and soul
I keep feeling this sensational thrust
Running through me
This incredible energy keeps surging through my body
Being away from you has shown me that I am yours
My soul aches for you
Close your eyes and feel my love around you
My love is yours alone
My world lightens up
With a mere glance of you
I always have you
I always want you
And if I concentrate
I can hear your excitable voice

And feel it exciting me
You know how it feels
This desire is beyond us
I wake up in cold sweats
A fiend
Ready to kill for a hit
Willing to die for a hit
Oh ... it hurts so good
It wakes me out of my sleep

The Dance

I'm dying
A slow and painful death
I hope and pray for the one thing that sets me free
And kills me all at once
But I can't stop
When it fills me
Joy embraces me
Repeatedly
While hell tugs at me
Completely
Everyday another piece of my soul dies
And every time I get what I so desperately want
It poisons me
I keep losing ...
And every time I lose
Something horrific happens
Not just to me
To the very core of my being
I can feel it, and yet, there is no end in sight
I have been staring into darkness for so long
I'm going blind ... maybe I deserve it
I've been preaching goodness for so long while dancing
That I failed to realize that my partner was the devil
The longer my death takes

The more likely he is going to win
I keep losing …
I must find a way not to get lost in the misleading comfort
Found in the lull of the dance
And practice what I preach

Pain

I thought I knew pain
On many levels
I've felt, seen and distributed my share
I have experienced extreme highs
Devastatingly extreme lows
But this …
This is some out of this world type hurt
I mean …
I truly never knew I could be so hurt … this hurt
I am completely and utterly devastated
I'm so bad that every inch of my body feels it
It's weighing me down
So I struggle
This pain is so deep
I don't even have to acknowledge it
Only to wake and be forced to recognize the pain
It lives behind the extra puffy eyes due to a tearful sleep
I struggle
I have felt lost and alone
Simply watching my life
No longer living it
How disrespectful
I struggle
I'm struggling with an unreal weight

This weight is so intense and intimately internal
It's potentially destructive
Surely this is no natural heaviness
It's misguided wicked influence
The prince of darkness knows I am divine
That's why he lurks in my madness
The devil likes when I'm weak
But I know he's a liar
Daily I must convince myself of what feels inconceivable
Part of me is dead and worst
Evil is trying to use that lifeless part to kill the rest of me
I struggle
God just wants me to lean on Him
I have to rely on what I have always known
God gives you what you need to survive
*Even if I don't know what **IT** is*
It's here, in me
It's my job to struggle through
And so I struggle
Eventually I'll win because God is good
I'm going to use this unique pain
Its distinct signature will elevate me toward an unforeseen destiny

Change

I have changed
I am barely recognizable to myself
Great tragedy
Alters beings
I am forever changed
There is goodness in the new me
I am disconnected from this world I live in
Thankfully
I am growing in spirit
I am stronger
Wiser
Less
And more than I have ever been
People no longer know me
It scares them
Sometimes I don't know myself
I have lost many
While gaining others
All I know is I have a choice
Options are always good
I can stay lost in my misfortune
Or be found in new strength
That is truer to who I now am
I am still becoming
And the journey ahead looks great

Guy Five

Awakening

Awakening

It

I have been searching for it
For a long time now
I don't even know what it is
And yet
I know that I am crazed without it
So I have continued my search
Through restless nights and raging moments
Only to find you have it
So my spirit is calm and happy with you

Love

In telling you this
I am trusting you
Trusting you not to hurt me
Trusting that your love for me
Will push forth your best
With regards to me
Not the worst
Unfortunately for me
There is nothing you can do
That could make me stop loving you
My love is all about you
Yet completely independent of you
It is unconditional
And simply amazing

Best Friend

I love the way you look at me
Your eyes pierce my soul
And when you hug me
You linger
Holding me near
Your kiss
Three times amazing
Our connection is visible
Yet unspoken
We are comfortable in our extended skin
You are my best friend

Good Love

Loving you has changed me
I am a better person with you
You have forced me to realize
That love should not be painful
Yes there are bad times
Due to life
Not each other
You have broken down walls I didn't know existed
You nurture my soul
And have helped me grow
Fear no longer resides in this heart
I love you

God's Gift

You were given to me
During a time when I needed you most
God allowed you to hold me
You appeared strong when I was weak
You are my divine connection
You strengthen me without trying
And continue daily
Your love not only fills me
It completes me
And makes me better
This is a unique love
Truly unconditional

Inspiration

I have a new perspective on life
I look forward to things differently
I want to experience life with you
While the future is uncertain
I have taken on the attitude of the time is now
You have inspired me
To embrace what God has given
We do not know what tomorrow brings
But with you
I want to find out

Heaven

He is heaven
My heaven
My personal angel
My divine connection
He guides me with his heart
His eyes are perfection
Those beautiful eyes
They pull me into his world
The world I want so desperately to be apart
I wish to return to my heaven
Continuously
But I will wait
To see if heaven is with me

Your Love

I don't need your love now
Don't get me wrong
I want it desperately
But I don't need it
I will want your love
When you know how much you love me
I will want your love
When you know that I have become a part of you
A good part
That is great with the other part that is you
I will want your love
When you have gained the knowledge
That I cannot be pushed away
I will want your love
When you feel there is no reason to test me
I will want your love
When you know intensely that I won't leave you
I will want your love
When you trust me as much as you need me to trust you
I will want your love
When you know that I won't willingly hurt you
I will want your love
When you acknowledge that you have longed for me
I want your love

Because we have waited for each other
I want your love
Because we have asked God
And His answer is clear
Our old selves may not have deserved this
But I want your love
Because of who we are together
Because of who we will be once we embrace this holy union
Better in every way
I want your love
Because WE deserve each other

Conclusion

Looking back, I now realize that I have never before been in a positive loving relationship. Through life's wonderfully naive moments I thought I had loved and been loved, but no. I was experiencing what I believed to be love. I must return and build on what I learned when I was younger, which is God is love. I have always believed in God, but there is a big difference in doing what you are taught to do and truly believing, acting and living in faith. There is a difference between thinking you know something and really knowing it.

Thankfully, my love of God and ever-strengthening spirit has allowed me, for the first time, to be in a position to receive real love. God is first in my life and His spirit feels me in such a way that it is affecting everything I do. God's love commands me to exist in a respectful manner and relationships. I am open to seeking out a love that will not only respect me, but also positively reinforce who I am, as well as who I am becoming. This love will nurture my soul, as well as make me a better person.

I believe that true love is an unconditional state of adoration and respect that cannot be waved. It is infallible and without reason that transcends the test of time. There is literally nothing that can be done to disrupt your union. True love is a truly divine connection that is simply beyond its participants. A spiritual relationship, which may thrust two people into an undying bond with God is true and each person becomes better because of it. Real love is holy and wonderful. Once this is understood, anything less is unacceptable. I will leave you with this thought found in the concluding poem—all people deserve to be loved and appreciated.

Appreciation

Appreciation is simple and essential to any good relationship
It is not something to be given or taken lightly
After all
It is someone's positive reinforcement of their admiration for another
Anyone deserving enough to be in your presence deserves at least that
I deserve to be appreciated
Do you?

Poem Index

Aching Soul. 28

Appreciation 47

Best Friend 39

Bleeding Heart 20

Change. 34

God's Gift 41

Good Love. 40

Heaven 43

How 12

Inspiration 42

It 37

It Was Never Love 21

Jennifer. vi

Last Night. 27

Love 38

Making Love. 4

More of the Same. 25

My Girls . . . . *viii*

Pain *32*

Seeing You *6*

Still *9*

The Dance *30*

The Man I Love *5*

Tomorrow *13*

Touching You *11*

Touch Me *10*

True Blessings *19*

Untitled 1 . . . . *17*

Untitled 2 . . . . *18*

Waking Up *3*

Why . . . . *xiii*

Why You're So Important *26*

Your Love *44*

Picture Index

Awakening 36

Distant Love 8

Distractions 16

Revelations 24

The Beginning 2

Introduction Picture xii

978-0-595-44750-3
0-595-44750-3

Made in the USA
Lexington, KY
12 April 2018